Fountain of Inner Joy

An Anthology of Lectures on Finding True Happiness

by Dr. T. R. Khanna
U.S.A.

Second Edition: 5000 Copies

Published by the *Wisdom Publishers Organization,*
a non-profit corporation dedicated to the publication
and promotion of universal wisdom.

http://WisdomPublishers.org
Email: Aditya@world.std.com

This book can be ordered at:

ShareLight.com or by sending your check or money order to the
Wisdom Publishers Organization at P.O. Box 8676, Lowell, MA 01853

ISBN 0-9727185-0-8 10.00

Price: $10.00 USA

Table of Contents

Foreword

Along with food, clothing, and shelter, happiness is one of our most basic human needs. In an attempt to satisfy that need, we tend to spend our free time seeking happiness in the pleasures of life: entertainment, eating, making more money, buying more things, making new relationships, seeking new thrills. But the problem with pleasures is that they are short-lived. In the moment, they may provide some enjoyment, but that enjoyment always fades away over time. Then we must seek additional pleasures to regain our happiness.

We seldom realize that the happiness we seek in temporary things can only be temporary. As we continue to search for lasting happiness by trying new and different pleasures, we continue to experience the same letdown after every attempt. Sometimes we intensify our thrill-seeking habits to the point of self-destruction, because we cannot find "that certain something" which will satisfy the basic human desire to be happy.

If we want to be truly happy, we need to change our understanding of the mechanics of happiness. Real happiness does not come from reaching outside of ourselves for the pleasures of this world. Real happiness comes from detaching ourselves from all the distractions of the gross world, and connecting our consciousness to the highest single aspect of our existence: the Fundamental Creative Life Force within us. That is the Fountain of Inner Joy.

In this anthology of lectures, Dr. Khanna explains the primary requisites of Inner Happiness. With simplicity and depth, Dr. Khanna explores the character traits which help us connect to our inner happiness, as well as the habits we must overcome to maintain that state of being. These talks contain many precious gems of universal truth, as well as practical exercises we can do to apply these truths in our daily lives. With earnestness and sincerity, the practitioner who applies him-or-herself will find the wisdom in this handbook to be a life-changing tool for many years to come.

Dr. T. R. Khanna, professor and lecturer, is a renowned Vedic scholar. He has authored numerous articles and several books, including an exposition of the Isha Upanishad and a concise elucidation of Patanjali's Yoga Sutras. He holds Doctorates in Philosophy and Literature, and a post graduate degree in Journalism. Dr. Khanna has taught Eastern philosophies in American universities and colleges since 1960.

All quotes in this book are from the lectures of Dr. Khanna.

Become the fountain of joy and compassion, showering love, understanding, and care.

Inspiration is the first step to happiness.

On Inner Happiness

Living in inner happiness is a commitment we make to ourselves the moment we get up in the morning. Unless we maintain inner happiness, we will look for happiness outside of ourselves in material things, events, or other people. If we are always waiting to be happy, real happiness will elude us.

Do Simple Practices

Everybody does external work—fixing their houses, cars, and material goods—but very few people fix themselves internally. If we improve inwardly, then we will project positive energy and happiness. We have to start with simple practices to make ourselves inwardly happy.

Be Grateful

Being grateful is the number one practice we should have. We should be grateful that we have this human incarnation, and that we are capable of introspection and self-development. We were not born as a monkey, fish, or other animal that is limited by instinct and governed by stimulus and response. We are in a human body!

Be Positive

We should have good mental practices. We should start the day with positivity, because we're going to spend the rest of the day with ourselves. The moment we get up, say to ourselves, "It's going to be a good day, no matter what. I'm going to give out good energy to the people I'm with today. I'm going to be happy and positive."

Start a Good Program

To gain inner happiness, we also need a good, practical program for health. A good program starts with us. Just as no one can eat for us, no one can have a good health program for us.

Early in the morning we should begin with aerobic exercises, or yoga stretches and breathing. To make our body strong, we can do weight training. We don't have to work on our body all day, but how we get up and how we start the day will make a difference.

Stay in the Absolute Feeling

We have to let go of our mental ups and downs. When things don't go exactly our way in daily life, we tend to think negatively. We amplify our own disappointments by our negative thinking.

We forget that victory or defeat happens in the mind. Bad or good vibrations happen in the mind. Whatever we are practicing inside is revealed on the outside, and in our interactions with others.

We cannot depend on gross feelings and outer stimuli for our happiness. We should practice having only one feeling—the Absolute feeling of inner happiness that comes from soul consciousness (*Aatam Vishvaas*). That's how we can have self-confidence and be ready to give happiness, instead of looking for happiness from others. We must realize that sometimes other people are busy. Sometimes, other people are not happy. They may have physical ailments, emotional pain, or be involved in their everyday problems of life.

We need to reduce our expectations about what others should give to us. These expectations are created by our own mind. If we are inwardly centered, we can give to others, rather than take from those who have their own problems.

If we are focused and together inside, we will do our best. We have to let go of ego, internal conflicts and expectations. If we stay connected to that Absolute feeling regardless of circumstances, failures and successes, then we'll be stable and happy in life.

Project Inner Happiness

Throughout the day, we should remain focused on positivity and inner happiness. Positivity is very contagious. We have all seen that when we are a little sad and we are with positive people, our own outlook improves.

When we are inwardly happy, we always have something to give. When we give happiness to others, it comes back to us. But if we are negative, that negativity colors how we perceive the environment around us.

We have to practice giving out good vibrations and encouragement to others. We should use kind words in abundance. If we have wisdom or good advice, we should share it. If we have some physical energy, we should do some good work or service. Whatever we can give, we should give. Our inner happiness shows in our acts of kindness and helpful attitude.

*We are very poor
when we seek
happiness in
things.*

*We are very rich
when we seek
happiness in
consciousness.*

Soul is
eternally
positive.

It is the
energy of
the Creator
in us.

Soul-Searching

Who are we? How can we know our true nature? One who is soul-searching asks these questions.

Soul-searching is not daydreaming, analyzing, or brooding. It is introspection into our real nature and the real purpose of life. Real soul-searching is reflecting on how we can change for the better. A mind left to itself can succumb to negativity. Soul-searching means separating ourselves from this tendency. It is realizing that we are not the negative thoughts and feelings that arise in our mind.

From the moment we get up in the morning until we retire in the evening, we have to stay inspired. The choice is clear: either we can become a victim of mental or physical laziness, or we can become an instrument of energy and inspiration.

Soul is the Absolute Feeling
of energy, peace, and inspiration
which sustains our total well-being.

If we form the habit of doing good for our mind, body, and soul from the moment we get up, we will not get involved with our gross feelings and mental waves. Then we will remember to do the good work for which we were given this human birth.

Soul-searching is reminding ourselves all the time that we are the energy of consciousness, a particle of the Creator's energy. It is plain lethargy when we are not inspiring ourselves. We can do a lot of activities with the body, but if we have not moved our mind to inspiration, we are mentally lazy.

We should never allow our mind to have negative self-talk. Instead, we should turn the mind to a positive awareness of soul and positive feelings based on soul-consciousness.

Rich is the person who ennobles his life with good qualities, good behavior, pure vibrations, and the depth of wisdom.

When we fill ourselves with the positivity that comes from the energy of consciousness, we will have a happy and prosperous life. Prosperity is not just having a lot of material things. We may not have millions of dollars, but if our attitude is positive and invigorating, we are very rich. We are endowed with Creative Intelligence. We can use that intelligence to answer the questions which soul-searching asks:

"Who am I? Am I these mental waves?
No!
Am I my negative emotions?
No!
Am I this gross body?
No!"

"I am the light of the soul,
the energy of the Creation."

*There is
no end
to joy
when we
put out
good energy.*

Directing Our Energy

Energy pervades this entire universe. Even empty space is teeming with energy. Galaxies are huge swirling masses of energy made up of millions of stars, and every star, including our own sun, explodes continually with tremendous amounts of energy. The sun's energy has been heating and lighting our solar system for billions of years. All life on earth depends on the sun's energy.

That same fantastic energy which explodes within our sun and permeates this universe is also within each of us. Energy makes our hearts pump, our eyes see, our ears hear, and our vocal cords speak. Energy illuminates our minds. Whether we are aware of it or not, we have a huge reservoir of energy within us. The quality of our lives depends on how we direct that energy.

Taking Charge

Every day we have the opportunity to become better and more vibrant human beings. For this, we have to use our energy creatively. Creativity in this sense is not just being able to fashion a beautiful sculpture or painting. Creative energy means being able to fashion our own lives to bring forth harmony and virtue. It means gracefully facing all challenges without succumbing to self-doubt, discouragement, and negative thoughts and feelings that deter us from reaching our potential.

When we direct our energy to uplifting thoughts, attitudes, and actions, we improve the quality of our lives. We create beauty for ourselves and our loved ones. We become healthy, happy, and stable. In contrast, if we let our energy go in the direction of self-pity, self-doubt, anxiety, and other negative manifestations, our own energy backfires on us. Negativity depletes our energy and taxes our immune system, making the body and mind more susceptible to disease. The overall quality of our lives deteriorates. In short, when we focus on our own negativity, we really abuse our energy.

Recharging Our Energy

If we are often negative or lethargic, we must deliberately change our ways. How? First, we can learn to recharge ourselves physically, mentally, and spiritually. We can recharge ourselves physically and mentally by exercising regularly, eating pure food, and avoiding anxiety and self-destructive habits. Exercise recharges us in the same way that running the engine of an automobile recharges its battery. Pure food helps us just as high quality fuel helps the performance and maintenance of an automobile. We have to learn to respect our body and adopt habits that support good health. We can't wait until tomorrow to begin a good health program. We must start today.

The foundation of our mental and physical health is spiritual health. Our spirit or soul is the life force at the core of our being. When we neglect that force, we jeopardize our mental and physical health. Just as we have to eat every day to maintain the strength of our body, we also have to feed ourselves spiritually every day to maintain the inspiration and strength of our character. Whatever inspires us recharges us. It connects us to the core of our being, the source of our inner strength and energy.

We can recharge ourselves mentally by reading inspiring thoughts and by making time for quietude and meditation every day. This is very important because our mind and senses are being constantly bombarded by stimuli: television, radio, the hustle bustle of the streets, pressure of the job, and so forth. Even if it is entertaining, all this stimulation depletes our energy. Without respite from this, we eventually become fatigued, and even depressed.

Going away on a vacation is not the answer. How often do we return from a vacation feeling like we need another vacation to recover? Vacations often do not bring us rest from the onslaught of outer stimuli; they just give us different stimuli. What we really need is to slow down inside and become peaceful. When we experience inner peace, our mind becomes quiet, our energy recharges, and our body heals. In effect, we get to that island of paradise without the expense or difficulties of traveling.

Shining Forth

In summary, all of us can channel our energy in a positive way. We just have to give ourselves a chance. We just have to give inner peace a chance. When we become peaceful and relaxed inside, our mind becomes focused and clear. With clarity of mind, we can experience that great reservoir of energy within us, the same energy that illuminates the sun and galaxies. We can direct our energy to attain the highest state of consciousness. Then, like the sun, we will bring brilliant, healing light to all those around us.

A deep person gives light wherever he goes.

If we have
control over
our mind,
we have
control over
our life.

Using Thinking as a Tool

Thinking, like fire, is a powerful tool which should be respected and used properly. We use fire to cook our food and heat our homes, but we must also contain and control that fire so that it doesn't burn down our house. Similarly, once we have thought through a problem and solved it, we should drop endless analytical thinking. If we continue in useless analysis, our thinking becomes a source of great stress.

When we repeat negative thoughts such as "Why did they do this to me," "It's their fault," "I am no good," or "I can't do it," we misuse and abuse our thinking. We should never allow negativity, selfishness, or confusion to become our regular way of thinking. Instead, we should control our thinking and use it for constructive purposes.

To control our thinking, we must detach ourselves from our own thinking processes. If we cannot find a solution to a problem, continuously analyzing the problem will not help us. Instead, we should stop thinking, step back from the situation, and gain a more objective perspective. Very often, this means giving up our point of view and our opinions so that we can see what is best for all.

We should think about the welfare of those with whom we live, and about the environment in which we live, and stop thinking so much about ourselves. As soon as we stop thinking selfishly and negatively, we can start directing our thoughts to positive activity. Then the tool of thinking comes under our control.

Controlling our thinking does not happen automatically. It is a daily practice. Each day we have to direct our minds to think in short, positive sentences that reinforce inner peace, goodness, and self-esteem. We should repeat thoughts such as "I am happy," "I can do this," and "My mind is a channel of pure, selfless energy."

The more we direct our minds to positivity, the more our actions reflect those good thoughts. When we become peaceful and balanced, our minds open to the creative energy of consciousness. Then we can use our thinking constructively to solve the problems of daily life. Problem solving is the right use of thinking.

When we use our thinking properly, it gives us the inspiration to do good actions. It allows us to solve problems quickly and efficiently. When our thinking process is positive and clear, we obtain optimum results with a minimum amount of energy.

There is tremendous energy in our thinking. When it's under our control, it becomes an asset. We become established in higher consciousness rather than in our intellect. Then we can use the tool of thinking efficiently and creatively, as a channel of Divine energy. We become very energetic and alert, our faculties become clear, and we use our thinking to its fullest capacity. This is the correct use of our thinking.

When thinking becomes prominent, joy fades away. When thinking disappears, the process of illumination begins.

Useless thinking is like blending water. It takes a lot of effort, but it accomplishes nothing.

When we open our hearts to God, our thinking becomes very simple and straightforward.

If we are going to think about anything, we should think about what we have been taught and how we can put it into practice.

It is a
very active
process to
attain inner
peace.

Take Time for Reflection

Most of us are usually very busy doing the activities of daily living such as working, studying, or caring for our family. The problem is that we seldom slow down long enough to consider how our life is going, and what we can do to improve it. We go, go, go, depleting our physical and mental energies with excess analysis, stress, and anxiety. Yet, if we made time for reflection, and gave inspiring and healing thoughts to ourselves, we could *gain* more energy to put back into our families and our lives.

Reflection means to meditate upon what we need to change or improve, and on what good we are doing and should continue to do. Taking time each day for reflection makes us deep, and gives us a feeling of stability that we don't get from just going through the motions of life.

Here are a few reflection techniques. Find a clean and quiet place where you can give yourself an hour every day to devote to meditative reflection. If you say, "But I don't have an hour to myself," try a half hour or take several fifteen minute breaks throughout the day. If necessary, tell your family what you are doing so that you won't be disturbed. Don't go to sleep during that

21

time. Practice a relaxation technique, such as Yoga breathing. Inhale and exhale slowly and deeply, being conscious of the air passing in and out of your nostrils. Slow down all mental activities, and curb all sensory interactions. During that time, there should be no eating, no music, no entertainment, and no conversation. Just close your eyes and sit quietly with yourself.

Another technique for reflection is to read inspiring quotes or books of wisdom. Then take time for introspection. Write down the things that you need to work on, and the things that you have learned. Read them over. With reflection, you get in touch with the core of your being, your inner spirit, and become aware of habits which may cause problems in interacting with others. For example, if you have been angry with someone or have spoken arrogantly, after reflection, go to that person and say, "I'm sorry. I didn't mean to say that to you." This kind of action weakens negative and egotistic habits. After practicing reflection, you will find that you can have a positive impact on whatever situation you are in, even though it may be a most trying one.

Take time for reflection. Reflection gives us freedom from the distraction of mundane preoccupations. When we are reflecting, we are not worrying. We are getting in touch with our focused, positive, relaxed inner state. Reflection is a creative process by which we enrich our spirit.

We must take some time off for purification of our soul.

Otherwise our whole life will go in counting our pains, worries and excuses.

If we can live with ourselves peacefully, we can face any challenge in life.

Face the Challenges of Life

We all have challenges in our lives. Driving a car or working at a job each day is a challenge. An emergency or crisis situation is a challenge. Living each day energetically and happily is a challenge. For some, even breathing is a challenge.

Whatever the challenges may be, our attitude and behavior determine how we deal with those challenges. When we are inwardly strong and firm with our mind, we can cope with the challenges of life gallantly, courageously, and happily. But when we succumb to the negative tendencies of our mind, we are overcome by them. We lose everything good in our lives, and we live in a very sorry state.

When a challenge comes, we should not be tense or stressful. We should turn our stress and tension into energy so we can face challenges with enthusiasm. If we are in a boat and it capsizes, we have to swim to shore. We have no other choice. Everyday life is like that. We have to face the challenges that arise. We really can't afford to quit.

None of us has the right to fall apart at a challenge. The human body is an amazing instrument. It has an enormous amount of resilience. As long as we have courage to face obstacles and difficulties, the body can overcome all kinds of hurdles.

Controlling the mind is also necessary in facing challenges. For example, if we are tired, we should not get annoyed. We should accept the fact that the body gets tired at times, and may need rest. Then we should rest. But we also should not escape into tiredness when we are really just lethargic or bored. The biggest hurdle in life is our own mind, because it gives up easily on good things, or in times of challenge.

To prepare ourselves for the challenges in life, we must go beyond our limitations. We should improve our stamina, resilience, and perseverance. We should have tremendous stamina to overcome the weaknesses of our body and the cowardly attitudes of our mind. Then when the challenges come, we will handle them courageously. If we are putting out tremendous energy and enthusiasm in daily life, we will always come out ahead. We will find ourselves in a deep state of happiness.

Some people
make problems
out of nothing.

Some people
make problems
into nothing.

More people are killed by worry than by hard work.

Freeing Ourselves from Stress

Recent medical and scientific studies have proven that stress is closely linked to many physical diseases and mental disorders. Though most of us experience stress in one form or another, many of us are not aware of how we create stress, or how we can overcome it.

How We Create Stress

When we are under stress, we tend to blame our difficulties on someone or something outside of ourselves. But, in fact, we cause our *own* stress. When we develop unreasonable goals, look for recognition, or want life to turn out exactly as we planned, we set ourselves up for disappointment. With disappointment come frustration and stress. We become impatient, we react, or we take too many things personally. We let our feelings and emotions rule us.

If we constantly bombard our minds with anxiety, useless analysis, or complex thinking, we develop stress fractures of the mind. Unattended, these fractures can turn us into nervous wrecks. When the mind cannot handle the pain any longer, it passes it on to the body.

The body, in turn, develops chemical imbalances which can lead to a host of diseases. We may get headaches, stomachaches, backaches, high blood pressure, ulcers or heart problems.

These ailments are merely symptoms of the problem; they are not the root of the problem. The root of the problem is that we forget that we are souls. Instead, we begin to identify with our body, mind, or status. We give importance to that which is temporary, rather than to our soul which is truly important. If we learn to break this identification with our temporary nature, we can actively break free from the grip of stress.

Getting Rid Of Stress

Getting rid of stress entails weakening our identification with our body, mind, and gross accomplishments. If we look at our life from the point of view of eternity, we can see that all these things that we are proud of, or cling to, are insignificant. As we continue to reinforce this outlook, we free ourselves from the anxiety of gross existence.

To weaken gross identity, there are things we can do. We can read inspiring thoughts and incorporate them into our lives. We can train ourselves to be less self-centered, and more aware of the needs of those around us. We should also remember that the body is the temple of the soul, and not destroy it with bad habits.

By practicing wisdom and having good habits, we can make the body a fit instrument for experiencing our higher nature. When we live in that connected state all the time, we are automatically freed from stress.

When we are balanced, we take care of the needs of the moment, cooperate graciously with others, live consistently by the highest principles, and stay even-minded.

When we are in a state of balance, the mind is automatically subdued. It stops giving us trouble.

If we are balanced, we are always energetic.

One who has
self-control is
the master of
his own destiny.

Overcoming the Reactive Mind

Every day, life presents us with countless situations in which we must make choices. The choices we make are dependent upon our mental state. We can make each situation a success or a disaster, depending upon our ability to drop our ego-centered images in the moment, and instead, choose the vibrant energy of higher consciousness.

Without our connection to higher consciousness, we become reactive, because we cling to old familiar ideas that clash with reality. But if we remember that we have an unlimited reservoir of constructive and creative energy within, we can tap into that energy and experience self-confidence.

Why is it important to stay in touch with this higher state? Because we may think that we know a lot, since we have gone to school and learned a few things. We may even think we "have it all together" because we are succeeding on the material level or functioning well on the job.

But if, in spite of all this, we are identifying with our images and expectations, rather than our higher consciousness, we are bound to fall prey to our reactive mind. When we do things from the ego-centered point of view, even if they are good things, we are easily victimized by our reactive mind.

What Are the Signs of a Reactive Mind?

The reactive mind has its own agenda, and does not want anyone or anything to stand in its way. Sometimes it becomes hostile, arrogant, abusive, or even violent, because it cannot have what it wants, when it wants it. At other times, the reactive mind becomes haughty, retorts, and has to have the last word. It is ready to argue and make excuses for its faults, rather than correcting them. The reactive mind angrily walks out, sulks, and hopes that someone will come and placate or pamper it. If nobody does, it goes into self-pity.

Looking for appreciation and recognition, and having feelings of self-importance are symptoms of the reactive mind. The reactive mind becomes resentful when it does not get the attention it seeks. It becomes very individualistic, and refuses to let go of its images or cooperate with others.

We need to operate in this world from a state which is beyond ego and the reactive mind if we want to have a happy, peaceful, and stable life. The following suggestions will help us attain the rewards of overcoming the reactive mind.

Ways to Overcome the Reactive Mind

Take Charge of Our Attitude

What does a positive attitude do for us? When we are positive, we can put others at ease and bring out their best qualities. We can create solutions instead of succumbing to the conflict that follows reactions. Whenever we discover that we are reacting, we should make mid-course corrections, and tune back into our inner peace and depth. We are the producer and director of our attitude, so it is our responsibility to make it the best.

Set Realistic Goals and Expectations

Sometimes we set unreasonable goals for ourselves, or we think other people have expectations of us. Then we frustrate ourselves trying to fulfill those expectations. As a result of that frustration we can easily trigger the mind to react.

We can overcome this reactive state by being more realistic in our expectations, and by letting go of those expectations where necessary. We should ask ourselves daily, "What kind of unreasonable demands am I creating that are making me react to situations and people?" Then we can create priorities that reflect more realistic expectations for ourselves and others.

Slow Down Inside

When we worry about how to accomplish our "to do" lists, we build a mental pressure cooker inside our mind and fuel it with more and more tension. It does not take long for our hyperness and tension to spill over into mental reactions.

To overcome reactive mental states, we need to learn to slow down the racing mind. To accomplish this, we can slow down our breathing, making each inhalation and exhalation deep and full. We can also put a brake on the racing mind by practicing hatha yoga poses with full concentration.

Practice Self-Improvement

If we really want to free ourselves from the reactive mind, we have to make a solid effort to do good actions and think good thoughts. Every day we should do something to improve our inner and outer environment. For example, we can start a new exercise program, go on a diet, or learn to meditate. By building confidence in our higher consciousness through self-improvement, we can learn to go beyond the reactive states.

Communicate Patiently

Whenever we are having difficulties, we should keep our communication channels open. Closing in and giving others the silent treatment, or blowing up and "letting off steam" is a false mental release which does not resolve any problems. By making an effort to be more patient with ourselves and others, and using a tremendous amount of love and care, we can explain things without reacting. We can learn to patiently tell others what our difficulties are, rather than expect them to know what is going on with us.

Give Encouragement

Sometimes we immediately react or criticize our loved ones without remembering our love for them. To avoid alienating our loved ones we should encourage them to be the best they can be instead of constantly criticizing them.

We should use kind words in abundance with our loved ones. Be quick to praise and slow to criticize. Good will and encouragement help everyone. In addition, we should avoid reacting or being critical at home, while at the same time, being overly friendly with outsiders.

Become the Observer

We can halt the reactive mind in an upsetting situation by becoming an objective witness. No matter how dire the situation is, we should remain calm, cool, and collected. Then we can take the necessary action from the perspective of inner clarity rather than outward panic. By becoming an observer rather than a participant in reactions, we can disassociate ourselves from the reactive mental state. We can calm down, listen carefully, and dissipate our own reactions while we let the other person have their say.

Be Compassionate

If people are trying to fight with us, we should give them help, rather than giving back our negativity. We should show them that there is a way out of their difficulty. We should be compassionate to help, and at the same time tough-minded to avoid reacting. Controlling our reactions to people who are reacting is very hard to do, but it becomes easier the more we draw upon our inner reservoir of compassion.

Beyond the Reactive Mind

Overcoming the reactive mind is not a one-time effort, it's a daily practice, a lifetime process. We should never give up on ourselves, nor should we underestimate the goodness we have inside. *Even one good practice can start to free us from the reactive mind.* We should keep working to develop that deep, intuitive, compassionate perception that comes from learning wisdom and practicing wisdom in our daily lives.

As our intelligence becomes established in wisdom and our practices reflect our higher consciousness, the mind automatically identifies with our real nature and our reactive tendencies are eradicated.

If we are
strict with
our mind,
we can be
at ease with
ourselves.

No negativity
will ever take
us to the best
of our potential.

On Grudges

What Is A Grudge?

From time to time, we have probably all felt grudgeful towards others. Quite often we hold grudges against others because our feelings have been hurt. But what we do about our grudges determines our future health and well-being.

There are two major factors that cause us to carry grudges: negative feelings and misunderstandings.

Negative Feelings

Grudges usually come when we are already feeling negative. If we are positive and energetic, we don't have time to hold grudges; we are too busy doing good things for ourselves and others. Instead of holding grudges, we should pick ourselves up and inspire ourselves to move forward.

Misunderstandings

From time to time, everyone makes mistakes. But holding a grudge against someone else because of a mistake is punishing ourselves. The other person may have already resolved the mistake he or she made and moved on to make a solid improvement. But we continue to waste our time and energy by holding a grudge. Instead, we should shun this self-defeating attitude and cultivate understanding and compassion. Then we can learn from other people's mistakes and move on with good energies.

Guidelines

To really drop our grudges takes time and constant effort. The grudges we have practiced for so long probably won't leave us overnight, but there are a few things we can do to change.

- *Drop it*—the moment we feel a grudge rising, just let it go. Not giving energy to a budding grudge is a lot easier than digging away at deep-rooted grudges. We should learn lessons from the successes and the mistakes of others, but throw our grudges away as though they are poison. If we carry grudges, we forget the lessons. If we remember the lessons of life, we never have to carry another grudge.

- *Forgive*—when we see ourselves and others as souls, we will not fall prey to the treacherous trap of grudges and hatred. We will apply understanding and forgive them.

- *Stop*—We should stop concentrating on other people's faults and start working on self-improvement. It's a lot more fulfilling and much better use of our time and energy. Grudges disappear when we work on removing our own faults. If we want others to drop grudges, we must be the first to get rid of our own.

- *Practice*—We must practice positivity. How can we hold a grudge against someone when we are thinking good thoughts and staying busy doing good things for ourselves and others?

- *Learn, don't burn*—Grudges heat us up inside and make us physically and mentally sick. Yesterday's grudges become today's problems, and tomorrow's chronic sickness. Learning, on the other hand, keeps us healthy, young, and vibrant, whether we are 16 or 60!

If we change ourselves, we have changed the whole world. If we don't change ourselves, we can change the whole world, and still we won't be happy.

Compassion,
rather than
annoyance,
should be
foremost
in our
interactions
with others.

Nurturing

Everyone needs care and nurturing for health, growth, and life itself. We all have been both the nurtured and the nurturer at some time in our life, and have experienced how uplifting it is. We all have seen how a mother takes care of her children or how a gardener tends to his plants. We have seen how compassionate and kind some nurses are to their patients. These are all examples of nurturing.

A broader perspective

In the broader sense, what does nurturing mean? Along with giving care on the physical level, nurturing means to care for life in the spiritual sense. It means to expand soul consciousness, spiritual understanding, depth, and stability.

Nurturing is sharing knowledge, and helping one another elevate consciousness. When we care and nurture, we create understanding so that our loved ones can have a healthy and happy life.

Nurturing can include helping others become aware of the consequences of their habits. For example, if we explain to people that inactivity leads to disease, or negative thinking leads to anxiety, they may be inspired to improve their habits or thinking patterns.

Show by example

We also nurture when we show others, by our own example, how to live with wisdom, health, and awareness. Our life teaches more than our words.

Hence, to be good nurturers, we ourselves have to have good physical, mental, and spiritual practices. We can't just want others to take responsibility for themselves; we must first be responsible for our own behavior and vibrations.

Beyond feelings

Nurturing is filled with sensitivity and compassion, but it has nothing to do with feelings and emotions. Feelings are just favorable and unfavorable sensations coming from fluctuations of the gross mind. When people's feelings are favorable, they happily give. But, when their feelings are unfavorable, they either grudgingly help or don't help at all.

To be good nurturers, we have to go beyond both favorable and unfavorable feelings. How? By connecting to true compassion. True compassion is not a feeling, but a state of being. It comes from Supreme Conscious-ness. It means having mercy, patience, and forgiveness.

When we have compassion, we don't become negative or react if our nurturing is not accepted. We are able to inspire, motivate, and give appropriate advice at an opportune time.

For example, if our loved ones have been advised to follow a low-fat diet, but have a weakness for high-fat foods, we need to help them follow the doctor's advice. We can encourage them to eat the right foods and help them understand the benefits of the new diet. A nurturer is like a doctor who focuses on healing the patient, regardless of his own or the other person's feelings. When we bypass personal feelings and stay connected to Consciousness, we never lose the spirit of giving. We don't get discouraged and stop helping, even if those we are caring for are sometimes negative or are not motivated to improve. We make an effort to stay in Consciousness and keep helping, encouraging, and inspiring.

When we are true nurturers, we can deal compassionately with even the most difficult situations. Everyone benefits and life improves in the company of a true nurturer.

Nurturing is being in the vibration of the breath of the universe.

It comes from the essence of being.

The healing
process takes
place in inner
quietude,
with active
participation
in positive
attitudes and a
positive outlook.

Our Healing Potential

Healing is an attitude of positivity. Healing energies are very necessary to alleviate any problem on the physical, mental, or spiritual plane. In healing, we use the regenerative power within to bring the subtle, vibrant rays of cosmic energy into ourselves.

A total healing program does not treat just physical symptoms. When we heal only the body, healing is incomplete. We also need to heal the mind and create a positive healing attitude. When we go to a doctor, he asks us about our physical symptoms and treats them. Going to a doctor or taking medicine is an important part of healing. But the most powerful ally in healing is to tap the healing force inside of us.

Our attitude affects how we heal. Sometimes we put unnecessary pressure on ourselves by becoming too critical. We blame ourselves and say, "I did it to my-self," or get discouraged and say, "I'm not getting better." These attitudes block our healing potential and delay healing. We should never allow our mind to indulge in negative feelings or jump to negative conclusions.

We should let go of negative emotions such as fear, frustration, or anger that may arise because of illness.

When we add emotions to our pain, our pain increases. We should remember that pain comes to everyone, but suffering is optional. If we keep our mind free from negativity and fill it instead with positive feelings and a positive dialog, healing will take place.

To bring ourselves back to good health, we have to nurture a positive mental environment, facilitate positive solutions, and inwardly relax. In other words, we have to develop positive practices. Practices such as positive affirmations, meditation, relaxation and reflection will create harmony in our body, mind and spirit so we can joyfully heal.

Practicing deep relaxation helps us heal. We should not feel guilty because we take time to relax. We should give ourselves healing vibrations through meditation and healing music.

Taking time for reflection helps us heal. When we read wisdom or keep a diary of inspiring thoughts and insights, we are reinforcing our healing potential.

Another healing practice is practicing positive visualization and positive affirmations. This will create a positive mental dialog. We should never be hard on ourselves because we have physical difficulty. We should encourage ourselves to improve and have the utmost confidence in our healing potential. The more positive energy we give ourselves, the more we will heal.

Practicing healing techniques such as relaxation, exercise, positive affirmations, laughter, and healthy eating, creates a total healing environment in ourselves. If we maintain a healing force field through consistent practice, we will remain in touch with our healing potential. These practices should never stop, as long as we have breath in the body.

When we live in a healing force field all the time, not just when we have a health problem, we become a channel for healing ourselves and others.

─────────────────────

If we want to be healed, we have to start by dropping those thinking habits that are hurting us and replacing them with meditative thoughts.

If we want to be healed, we should not be affected by our mind or by the minds of others.

Every motion, every action, and every thought should be put into the healing process. We should avoid any negativity, and any negative suggestion in order to be healed.

To communicate, we need a little time, a little love, and great patience.

Congeniality

When we live together as a family, we should live as allies, not enemies. We should relate to each other on the highest level rather than take each other for granted, or worse, pull each other down. We should be congenial, and willing to cooperate. Our inclination should always be to perform kind and charitable acts, and give the benefit of the doubt to our loved ones when they are in trouble.

If we remain emotionally stable and balanced within, we will be ready to help our loved ones when they are having a problem. We can be their best ally by making ourselves focused, alert, and ready to help. We should encourage the highest tendencies and avoid making life unpleasant for each other. We should not disturb others by saying something unkind or harsh. But we also should not agree with them just because we are afraid to speak the truth. If we are vigilant about the quality of our speech, our vibrations, and our behavior, we can be congenial without sacrificing our principles.

Tendencies to Avoid

What are the tendencies we should avoid in ourselves in order to be congenial with the people we love? We should avoid being antagonistic, deliberately argumentative, or overly critical of others' imperfections. We should not be patronizing or try to make anyone feel inferior or degraded. We should not be easily provoked into anger or annoyance. We should avoid complaining. If we need help on something, we should politely ask for help. Congeniality doesn't mean participating in bad habits such as smoking, drinking, or eating meat because we are seeking acceptance. These habits will eventually cause disease, unhappi-ness, and problems for the family.

Qualities of Congenial People

Congenial people are easy to get along with. They are patient, and they do not get annoyed for every little thing. They are mature enough to respond positively rather than react, even when provoked. Their words are agreeable and wholesome, even when others are harsh with them.

Congenial people take care of their loved ones, so they have no time to complain about their own aches and pains. They are understanding and sympathetic without being overbearing. They are not boastful or arrogant. They have a friendly quality of humility about them. They are caring, courteous and loving. They harbor no jealousy or animosity. People who have mastered the art of congeniality are cheerful and compassionate. They share wisdom and advice un-grudgingly.

As *we* imbibe the qualities of congeniality, we strengthen our family relationships and improve our own social skills. Our openheartedness in thought, word and deed improves life for ourselves and our loved ones.

As we see the cream in the milk, the sweetness in the sugar, and the fragrance in the flower, in the same way, we should see the soul in one another.

Congeniality has nothing to do with superficial social norms. That's not congeniality, it's substandard behavior. The good standard for behavior is to become established in superconscious awareness of our Real Self.

Never
be afraid
to keep
speaking the
truth with
love.

Virtuous Speech

Those who have mastery over their speech are considered to be virtuous people. They fill their communication with wisdom and love.

These noble people are gracious and share wisdom ungrudgingly. They speak the truth lovingly and thoughtfully, devoid of egoism. People who have virtuous speech bypass any negative emotions and feelings when they give advice. They speak from the highest level of consciousness.

In speaking, timing and delivery are of utmost importance. We should speak only about what is necessary, and speak at the appropriate time. Our speech patterns, demeanor, and vibrations should be free of negativity, and our delivery should have no undercurrent of arrogance or hostility.

When speaking the truth, we should never speak out of annoyance. We should also avoid speaking with curtness, coldness, or arrogance. We should not knowingly annoy others, or make them nervous or uncomfortable. Hearing the truth may disturb some people, but their disturbance should not be caused by our delivery.

We shouldn't use undesirable language or pass underhanded remarks. We shouldn't be sarcastic, because sarcasm is a quality of ego. Remarks made with cruelty, jealousy, or animosity are like arrows which pierce another person's heart.

We should neither speak the truth harshly, nor speak a lie to please anyone. We can deliver the truth to others without disturbing our peace of mind. Truth which is spoken with an undisturbed mind and with pure motives frees us from mental turmoil.

We have to remember that what we are saying is for the other's benefit. But if they don't like hearing the truth and they react, we shouldn't take it personally. We should do our utmost to stay totally dispassionate.

If we really want to make a positive impression on others, we need to give wisdom, but explain it with love. We have to remain totally focused and use kind words in abundance. It's not just a matter of courtesy. It's a matter of heart—a truly compassionate heart. Having mastery of speech, filled with wisdom, is the sign of saintly people.

Being in the Absolute means always speaking the truth and never compromising with untruth.

Our good words never go to waste. Harsh words always become a source of regret.

The highest form of fellowship is Selflessness.

Living in Fellowship

Fellowship is the spirit of unity that comes from living on the highest level of soul consciousness. Fellowship does not mean pleasing others through charm or just giving personal attention to one another. It is the company of good, like-minded people who have come together to learn the highest wisdom and to encourage one another to grow.

We can only maintain fellowship by having the spirit of self-sacrifice and cooperation. It means guarding against tendencies which disintegrate unity and cooperation—tendencies which heighten ego fulfillment. Ego separates us from fellowship by making our individual needs and preferences seem important; whereas, in fellowship, we see the needs of the whole and encourage one another to expand consciousness.

Fellowship cannot be maintained by rules. Rules are made to control people who are individualistic. When individuality is rampant, we do not recognize the source of our strength and prosperity. Where there is fellowship, we realize that real strength comes from unity. We become willing to give up personal desires and motives for unity. We are united in soul consciousness. When we live in consciousness, it is natural to cooperate without breaking our principles.

We cannot function well in a cooperative situation if we are filtering everything through our feelings. When we are only thinking about ourselves, everything disturbs us. In fellowship, we go beyond our feelings in order to cooperate. Then we learn to see objectively what is good for all.

To sustain fellowship, everyone must work on self-improvement. When we are healthy, we can contribute more to the environment which sustains our lives and souls. When we improve ourselves, we are ever-ready to serve and cooperate for the good of all.

We have to look at life from the point of view of eternity. If we are eternal, then everything born of this gross body or of attachment to this gross body is temporary. If we forget that we are eternal, we get caught up in attachment to this body. Then our problems seem to multiply, and positivity disappears from our lives.

Cooperation and fellowship make this life sweet.

Wisdom is the source of solace, peace and prosperity.

Listen to the Wisdom
of a Wise Teacher

Gather around the high teacher who has deep perception and is actively pursuing wisdom and spiritual
perfection. Because that high soul is evolved in consciousness, he will help us gain wisdom, create positive
changes, and evolve in consciousness. Wise people have
sharp wisdom which surpasses all intellectual rhetoric.
They are extremely perceptive and their judgement is
very clear, because they thoroughly understand human
behavior. Knowing that much of the world is driven by
greed, selfishness, and ego, wise people witness other
people's tendencies, as well as their own, and do not
partake in them.

Highly evolved souls are simple and extremely capable,
and help bring about positive transformation in people's
lives. They are vibrant, focused, and active in
self-development. They enhance goodness in themselves—the study of wisdom, meditation, exercise, yoga,
pranayama—and try to bring goodness into the lives of
others.

Wise people who are pursuing the highest knowledge
set an example of inspiration, positivity and compassion. They are not fussy or complaining. They are

forgiving by nature. They have firm principles, yet are accommodating to make the best of every situation. Wise people are able to dissipate tension and conflict, because they do not give importance to ego.

If we want to experience the joy, ecstasy, and inner contentment that is beyond stimulus and response, we should pursue the path of Supreme Consciousness. When we meet a *true teacher*, he guides us to that Supreme light.

That is why we should gather around and support a high teacher, and adopt his universal outlook. We should learn from him in an environment where wisdom is freely given and people improve. With the guidance of such a wise soul, we can free ourselves from delusion and suffering.

If we want to attain the highest status in our lives, we must follow in the footsteps of the wise and the noble.

Humility is very
simple.

It is not an act.

It is a state
of being that
comes from
the heart.

The Power of Humility

When we are truly humble, we are relaxed. We are not dominated by attachment to our ego or egotistic points of view. True humility gives us strength because it removes pride from our personality. It has the power to open up a new dimension for us so that we can achieve awareness of our Supreme Nature. In this higher dimension, we experience our noblest qualities. In whatever studies we pursue, in whatever duties we perform, when we do them with humility, our ego is not in charge—we are. But in the absence of true humility, we become the victim of our own self-importance, shallowness, and desire for immediate gratification.

It is through the practice of wisdom, devotion, and dedication that we become pure-hearted, and free from ego. When we practice the quality of humility, we neither get puffed up nor depressed with a false sense of superiority or inferiority. Ego is basically an obstacle; whereas true humility frees us from arrogance, ignorance, and pride—everything which makes us weak.

We should understand that the power of humility is greater than the weaknesses of ego. In all our endeavors, we should manifest our divine nature through the practice of humility. The fullness of our Supreme Nature is derived from the egoless state, and the

egoless state is attained through harnessing the power
of humility.

———————————————————

Humility is very simple. It is not an act.
It is a state of being that comes from
the heart.

Humility is the first step to liberation.

Humility is an affirmation of the qualities of the soul, whereas politeness is
just a social etiquette.

Absence of ego is the passport to the
Absolute.

It is not important
how strong
we are.

It is important
how humble
we are.

Humility is
a quality
of strength.

Joy is the way of those who help themselves and others improve.

Be Joyous!
Be Grateful!

The moment we embrace the morning,
we should be grateful and
think about all the blessings
and all the amenities
that the Creator has given to us
in this human incarnation.

Whenever we start our day in prayer and gratitude to the Creator, we realize that this breath of life is a very precious gift. Even though we are but a little particle, we experience tremendous joy and happiness when we connect our consciousness to the beauty and the vastness of this creation.

When we *start* each day with joy and gratitude, we set the tone for the day. A good attitude helps us to meet the challenges of daily life. By projecting positive energies in our interactions with others, we can overcome negativity or adversity. The day is then spent with love, helpfulness, and happiness, rather than in criticizing or complaining.

With this simple exercise of getting in touch with our inner happiness, we automatically rise above the noises of the mind and its images. We *cannot* afford to get involved with the mind's idiosyncracies and demands. If we start the day on a fault-finding mission, we will waste the whole day complaining—making ourselves and others miserable. Instead, if we start the day on a good energy mission, we create a joyful life. We keep moving forward with gratitude for this human existence.

We should never lose gratitude for the inner light and the manifestation of that light around us.

Gratitude sparkles the heart!

BEYOND LIGHT IS ESSENCE, AND THAT ESSENCE IS TRUTH.

Remember the Essence of Being

Everything is born out of the Essence—the sun, the planets, the galaxies, and the space between them, the earth, the oceans, all living beings—everything. All that is creative, all that is positive, and all that is uniting in consciousness comes from the Essence of Being. We should remember that Essence under all circumstances, because that is what brings us liberation from the gross nature. Somehow, we forget the Essence and get caught up with the activities and images of day-to-day living. We identify with our name, form, status, and heritage. If we get subjectively entangled in things that are happening on the gross level, we sink into the quicksand of worldly existence.

While pursuing status and accomplishments, we lose peace of mind. Sometimes there is success and we are elated. Sometimes there is failure and we are depressed. But if we see this life as a dream, we can work hard without getting attached to success or failure. If we do our work without attachment to the results, it does not cause us pain.

When we remember our Essence, gross existence looks neither threatening nor attractive. The gross is only attractive or repulsive when we are mentally caught in the ups and downs of specific events. If we connect to our Essence all the time, then gross reality doesn't bother us.

Destroying the Ego Perception and Images

We need to weaken the potency of ego in order to attain permanent happiness and peace. How? We weaken ego through the practices of meditation, introspection, simplicity, and most of all, humility to the Essence of Being. Once we see ourselves as separate from our gross ego drive, we weaken its hold on us. When egotistic perception is weakened, then we are not tormented by worldly distractions or images.

Quieting the Mind

To remember our Essence, we have to quiet our mind. When we listen to the Om sound or deep silence in meditation, we forget the noises of the gross mind. As we stop the noises of the conscious or unconscious mind, we experience our Essence. Once we experience our inner peace and happiness, we won't get caught up in the gross reactions of our mind.

The most important daily activity we have is tapping into the energy of our Essence. All the vagaries and attachments of the mind leave us when we are full inside. When we remain focused on our Essence, we are able to face the challenges of this life.

The essence of
life is not in the
satisfaction of our
physical desires.

It is in giving
food to the
soul so that we
can unfold a
tremendous surge
of creative energy.

When we close the doors to our own ego we are free and happy.

Going Beyond
Ego Perception

We should constantly ask ourselves, "Who am I? What am I doing with my life? What is this worldly life about?" This self-analysis helps us to keep the perspective of consciousness in our daily life. It helps us see what is real and what is unreal, what is important and what is unimportant. It also helps us separate our true self from our gross ego, and to see ego clearly.

Ego is like a poison berry plant growing inside of us. Unchecked, it takes over and causes us a lot of pain and suffering. Ego makes us feel superior or inferior, excited or bored, reactive or complacent. When we are living in our ego, we end up carrying grudges, tension, and other negativity. Ego creates pettiness instead of open-heartedness. It superimposes itself on our higher feelings of forgiveness and compassion.

In ordinary consciousness, we filter everything through our limited perception of ego. We need to go beyond this limited perception in our thinking, attitudes, and conversation. When we raise ourselves to a higher level of consciousness, we no longer look for acceptance or feel rejected. We rise above negativity, reactions, and images.

When we go into higher consciousness, we do not get into mental conflicts with ourselves or others. Rather than resorting to blame or arguments, we find solutions congenially and compassionately.

Our challenge is to rise above ego feelings and negative energies. When we raise our thinking to a higher level, we go beyond our ego. Our thinking is clear, because it comes from higher consciousness.

Avoid ego reactions, not challenges.

Focusing the mind on our Absolute nature removes self-doubt and negativity.

Our Absolute Brilliance

The wisdom of the Vedas reminds us to keep the company of wise people, to have the same high thoughts, and to treat each other with balance, love, and wisdom. It encourages us to come together for one purpose: to experience our true nature, our Absolute Brilliance.

If we embrace our Absolute nature, we can attain and experience that brilliance —the light and awareness of our superconsciousness. In that high state we are living on the top of the mountain (our superconscious state), above all the excitement and pain of the polluted city, (our gross mind and images).

Our state of brilliance is achieved by staying focused on Absolute wisdom and Absolute understanding. In the brilliance of Absolute consciousness, we can never be troubled by daily trials or gross limitations. Our intelligence becomes superior, and our consciousness is sharpened. We see the flow of nature and energy and we live in that flow. We see beyond this gross existence.

If we want to experience the brilliance of consciousness, then we cannot be limited by our heredity, training, habits or culture. We must live in our timeless Absolute nature. We can be born yellow, red, white, brown, or black. It does not matter. We were born from the Absolute Brilliance and into the Absolute Brilliance we will merge.

People mistake the gross state of feeling good for the vibrant state of the Absolute. But the real joy, the real feeling of goodness comes from the ocean of Supreme consciousness. All creatures are living in this life due to the Supreme consciousness. We are sustained by that strong wave of bliss. Our small thinking cannot be compared to this. That is why we have to humble ourselves to God, to that sustaining energy.

That energy is beyond images; it is not in our limited perception about life, or about God. By our images of various religions we are limiting that creative regenerative force, because we are labeling it from our earthly point of view. That Supreme state cannot be limited by any name. It is untainted, untouched, and cannot be destroyed. And that state is within our reach, because it is within us!

Constantly evolving is being close to the Absolute.

To prepare
ourselves for
life's challenges,
we must go
beyond our
limitations.

Then, when
the challenges
come, we will
handle them
courageously.

Reaching Our Full Potential

We all want to become strong and reach our full potential, but we sometimes lack direction or drive. What stands between us and our full potential? How do we reach our potential? These are the things that we need to know.

Those who rise to great heights, whether in sports, business, leadership, or in spiritual development, have one thing in common: they have the courage to overcome complacency and reach their potential. Their unceasing effort to excel gives us an example to emulate. They have shown us that with perseverance and inspiration, we are just as capable of reaching our own potential.

Self-imposed limitations are the number one hindrance to reaching our full potential. We make excuses for our inadequacies. Although it seems easy in the moment to make excuses rather than to do something constructive, our excuses eventually catch up with us. Our excuses weaken the potency of our potential.

When we say things such as "I can't exercise because I am not athletic," "I cannot learn that because I am too old," or "I cannot work hard because I am not used to it," we are making excuses to remain complacent. Only by rejecting our excuses can we conquer our mental and physical inadequacies. If we adopt a program of regular exercise and good habits, we will not remain under the grip of our lethargic mind. Our slogan for reaching our potential should be "Find ways, not excuses!"

How To Reach Our Potential

The process of reaching our potential involves training and controlling the mind. It is not a process of struggling with the mind; rather, it is a process of guiding the mind to something better. One effective way to guide the mind is to be positive. For example, we should make it a daily habit to repeat positive affirmations such as "My potential is limitless,""I am very resourceful," or "I can learn anything I make up my mind to learn." By repetition of positive affirmations, we create positive impressions in our memory system.

We cannot, however, just be mentally positive. We have to become actively positive in everything we do. "Active Positivity" is what separates people who are doing from those who only think about doing. Positive action bridges the gap between having potential and living up to the fullest of that potential. To be a truly positive human being is to think positive thoughts, do positive actions, and stop our bad habits. If we constantly strive to make each moment the best, we build positive momentum in our lives. As each positive moment passes, it builds good memories so that we are free from the burden of past regrets.

As we develop the habit of taking positive action at every step in our lives, we experience something even greater than the joy of positivity. We realize that beyond the limits of our body and mind lies a powerful and positive resource of energy—the force of Consciousness, the force of soul. Nothing is greater than the strength of our soul. When the mind becomes positive, it automatically becomes a transmitter of our soul energy. Whatever is positive within us comes from the strength of soul. Whatever is self-defeating within us is the voice of the limited mind. Consciousness cannot be defeated. It is eternally positive. We have to tune into Consciousness by quieting our mind, meditating, and living up to our potential.

Applying Our Potential

In summary, to become strong and live up to our highest potential, we must stop making excuses and start inspiring ourselves. We need to create a solid program for ourselves so we can maintain good mental and physical health. We have to do good actions that improve the quality of our lives, the lives of our loved ones, and our environment. Most of all, we have to have great conviction in the strength of our soul, so we won't be defeated by any adverse circumstances or difficulties we encounter. Then, in spite of life's challenges, success will embrace us on the path to reaching our highest potential.

Peace descends when we stop seeking the fruits of our actions.

Perfected Action

The scriptures instruct us that our duty is to do good actions always without seeking the result of those actions. How can we do that? Good actions can only come from a pure heart and pure mind. When our hearts and minds are pure, then our actions are pure. The mind is purified when we fill it with wisdom. Then, the thirst for attaining results from our actions ends because we realize that good action is its own reward.

Let us suppose that we serve someone we love and he neither responds, nor does he return the service. We should not feel slighted or feel that our service has been wasted. We should be confident in our higher nature, whether our good actions are appreciated or criticized.

If we want to help our brothers and sisters, friends and relatives, but we get upset because they do not want our help, then we are not helping selflessly. Instead, we are wanting people to behave according to our images. That is called seeking the fruits of our actions. But when we bring wisdom into our lives, we become secure within ourselves and are not discouraged by other people's actions.

Instead, we should remember that we all have bad habits that are difficult to change. To change and improve daily we should keep inspiring ourselves and others to practice wisdom. Only by practicing wisdom do we gain detachment from our feelings and emotions. Then we are able to put love, joy, and good actions into our own and one another's lives.

When we renounce the fruits of our actions, all our pain ends because we no longer have expectations involved in our deeds. We are no longer looking for someone to accept our love. We are no longer looking to gain something from the other. If we tell someone the truth, we have done our duty, and they may gain from following the good advice.

For example, if we have relatives who tend to overeat, it is our duty to set a good example by not overeating. Also, we should explain to them that they are destroying their own health by eating too much. If they still overeat, and if we get upset, it means we are attached to fulfilling our own images, rather than really helping. We cannot walk away from our loved ones or stop giving help, but we *must* walk away from our attachment to our emotions. We cannot get angry because anger only fans the fire of dissension. It never inspires the other to change for the better.

In summary, we must renounce the desire for the fruits of our actions because desire leads to the duality of pain and pleasure. However, we must not renounce actions themselves because we have a duty to the welfare of our loved ones and to our own soul. When we renounce the fruit of our actions, we perform all actions clearly.

When we drop our own motives and expectations, then we are able to see clearly what is good for the other. When we stop worrying about the specific manner in which those results manifest, our pain ends. This is called perfected action and perfected action takes us to our highest state.

Inspiration and self-development are a full-time job.

Energize yourself with freshness every day, every moment, in every way.

Live in the Freshness of the Moment

It is very important that we always keep the conscious and subconscious mind fresh with the healing energies of Consciousness. Washing the mind with the vigorous, shining energies of Consciousness frees us from negativity, grudges, and false perception. As that freshness flows into us, it also manifests in our attitude and behavior with others, especially our loved ones.

Freshness creates harmony, and harmony brings peace of mind. When we foster harmony we are gracious, kindhearted, forgiving, and caring. How do we imbibe these qualities? By making a total commitment to our real self which is sitting inside us. That is who we really are! The shining light of consciousness inside of us is full of wisdom, vim, and vigor. If we let our real self come out, we will heal any negative feelings that we might have. We will overcome any obstacle and be able to contribute selflessly.

To start every day fresh, give yourself a daily dose of compassion. That means staying away from discouragement, anger, or reactions, because these negative states block compassion. We can become more compassionate by following this simple formula: practice kindness and forgiveness. Helping, adjusting, caring, and forgiving is an ongoing process that we should never stop.

Freshness in the moment is essential when we are helping people. It keeps us focused. What happens if we are not focused and peaceful? We can easily lose balance, and without balance we cannot help anyone.

Starting each moment and each day with freshness is very natural when we remember this: this whole world is a drama, and our gross mind is a drama. So why should we get caught up in our mentality play or other people's mentality play? Why should we get caught up in anyone's false ego-perception, including our own?

Each moment is new. Each moment is fresh. That is why we should not work in mental boxes. When we work in mental boxes, we lose flexibility and creativity. Who makes plans? We do. Who makes deadlines? We do. Our mental plans are nothing but shadows of the mind. Some are realized and some are not. If we always start fresh and maintain inspiration, we will add clarity and positivity to our lives and our environment.

When we live in freshness, no challenge is too big and no work is below our dignity.

Changing for the better begins with self-respect.

Change is the Challenge!

Transformation is constantly occurring everywhere in the universe. Some galaxies are just being born, and others are fading away to be recycled into new galaxies. Similarly, every day something in our life changes, transforms, is different in some way from the day before. If change is inevitable, then we should seek to make positive changes.

The sages have told us that the purpose of this human incarnation is to transform in consciousness, so that our lives change for the better. But transformation of consciousness only begins when we become aware of our weaknesses and faults. Until that realization comes, we are satisfied with the way we are, and make little effort to change.

Sometimes we do not accept that we need to change for the better because we think our problems are someone else's fault. We look for someone or something else to blame. But blame does not transform us. Blaming is simply an excuse we use to *avoid* changing. If we want to truly transform our lives, we should stop blaming and start listening to the good advice and deep wisdom which the sages and mystics have given us.

Wise souls can help us because they have already explored consciousness. They have confronted their weaknesses, self-centeredness, and negative feelings. They have overcome those hurdles to live in the freshness of Supreme consciousness.

When we listen to the wise and their wisdom, we can either take it personally and react negatively, or we can transform ourselves. If we think, "Who are you to tell me?", then we do not change. Our ego blocks listening. Instead of listening and practicing, ego wants us to deny our faults by making excuses, being in denial, or postponing change. But if we think, "Wow, what a challenge to my thinking!", then we are ready to move forward with the changes we need to make. We set aside ego and negative reactions, and happily accept the challenge to change.

If we want to live a happy and well-integrated life, we have to change now and move forward. It is useless to dwell on past mistakes or to live in wishful thinking about future change. We should become grateful for the goodness we already have, and actively seek ways to improve our lives in every aspect.

There is nothing greater to accomplish in life than our own transformation in consciousness. No one is perfect. But by accepting the challenge to transform in consciousness, day by day, we will gain the qualities of inner peace, depth, and happiness.

Changing for the better is an on-going process.

From the point of view of eternity, all problems are insignificant.

Living in our Eternal State

Living in our eternal state is a very freeing experience. It is a state of unending inner peace and balance. To live in that state, we have to eternalize ourselves, that is, inspire ourselves with the realization that we are eternal. We have to turn our mind inward and wash it with the depth of wisdom. Most of us are running outward to all kinds of distractions, events, people, food, and so forth. But if we learn to eternalize our outlook, our mind becomes healthy and happy.

What happens when we *externalize* our outlook rather than *eternalizing* it? An external bent of mind makes us preoccupied with pursuing gross trivial goals, rather than our spiritual growth. We mistakenly seek happiness through acquiring more things, more wealth, and more status. This goal of amassing more material things puts us under the constant pressure of having to maintain and protect them. We install security alarms or hire guards to save our possessions from thieves. But if we do not collect so many things in the first place, we can free our mind and time to focus on what is really important—protecting our soul.

Giving credence to the materialistic world is nothing more than self-deception. In that deception we cannot see our eternal nature or learn ultimate truth. We are like the thirsty traveler going through the desert. He sees something up ahead and thinks it is water. But when he arrives there, he finds that it is only sand.

If we want to be truly happy, we have to eternalize our outlook. We cannot just get caught up in the whirlwind of daily activities. We must do practices that help us remember our eternity. We have to train our mind to love wisdom. We have to take time to experience peace. We have to prepare ourselves for Eternity, not for the worries of this gross existence.

The only limitations we have are self-imposed. Soul is ever-free.

Constantly evolving is being close to the Absolute.

Millions and billions of years are nothing from the cosmic point of view, because the cosmic point of view is not affected by time and space.

Don't put limits on your positivity.

We start experiencing our Eternal nature when we go beyond our name and form.

You are...
You were...
You will be...

A particle of
Eternity.

True love resides
in our Spirit-Self
and is free from
the infection of ego.

True Love – A Quality of the Soul

True love originates in the Spirit-Self. It is seeing and loving others as souls. It sounds like such a simple concept, yet living it can be very difficult. Why is this so? Because our ego steps in and clouds our vision. The source of true love is the soul, not the ego. Ego wants to possess others, but no one can be possessed. If we don't even possess our own bodies, then how can we possess anyone else?

Due to ego, we pursue different images and different goals. When so many images clash, it leads to discord and unhappiness. We begin to develop unrealistic expectations of our loved ones; then cooperation and fellowship are relegated to the background. Eventually, love dies down and the family breaks apart.

It requires openheartedness with our loved ones to have cooperation and fellowship. If we aren't openhearted with our family, then with whom are we going to be openhearted? If we don't love our family members, and seek to impress people we don't live with instead, we haven't understood love.

Love is unity and cooperation, and that only comes when *everyone* is contributing to the welfare of the family. We cannot expect one mother to take care of the whole family while everyone else is off pursuing his own dreams, images and individuality.

The women of the family should not be treated as maids. They should be treated as souls. Where women are respected and happy, that household prospers. Where women are treated badly, even if there is money, that household is destroyed.

Where the soul flourishes, then love flourishes. But where love is buried under ego, we forget to treat each other as souls. Then there are harsh words and fights. If we wish to love and be loved, then we must start loving the souls of our family members and stop hurting them by expressing ego and arrogance in our speech.

Loving the souls of others starts with loving our own soul. It means to practice positivity and joy, to put enthusiasm into changing for the better, and then to encourage the best in our loved ones. True love *is* having selfless concern for the other's soul, the other's life, and the other's well-being.

By cultivating a spirit of universal love within ourselves, we create an atmosphere of harmony, cooperation, and mutual respect.

True love is commitment, loyalty, and sincerity in the good or bad times.

True love is all about giving without expectations.

Living in excellence is the highest challenge we can accept.

If we want to be extraordinary human beings, we have to do extraordinary things.

Living in Excellence

Excellence is a very special state of being. When we live in excellence, we manifest those qualities of mind and heart which make us extraordinary human beings.

Excellence comes from our connection to consciousness, that internal dynamo of creative, regenerative energy. This connection gives us soul confidence, the true confidence which helps us attain our highest potential.

Excellence does not come from what we accomplish on the physical plane of existence. Believing that our self-esteem is measured only by what we can achieve on the gross level comes from a shallow understanding of the human potential. This belief system can make us physically, mentally, and emotionally exhausted, whether we meet our own images of success or not. We should abandon that outlook and realize that it is improving our inner qualities which will help us live in excellence.

No one is perfect. Only God is perfect. Pursuing excellence does not mean that we should try to become perfectionists. Perfectionists are seldom happy, because they are too fussy. They try to make everyone and everything fit into their rigid mental boxes. Excellence is neither rigidity nor fussiness. It is a natural result of living in consciousness. Excellence is attained by putting out energy to be better than we were yesterday, rather than trying to be perfect.

What is the difference between an ordinary and an extraordinary person? The extraordinary person lives up to his own high standards. He doesn't make excuses, and he never puts limits on his excellence.

To do extraordinary things *we* have to believe in *our* extraordinariness. Pursuing excellence with this outlook kindles great creativity, and we feel renewed and invigorated.

Excellence and ego cannot co-exist, because ego is always looking for recognition.

We should make excellence, not mediocrity, our style.

Intensity for excellence is the hallmark of an extraordinary human being.

The extraordinary person does not need to follow the crowd.

Our true happiness comes from the Source which gave us existence —the Supreme. That is the source of true bliss, the embrace of Divine love. That is the source of fullness from within. From that Source comes the Fountain of Inner Joy.

Healing only takes place when we are emotionally balanced and mature.

Self-realization is freedom
from our own ego.

When our own ego is not
tamed, it becomes a
liability.

For an inspired soul, every
moment is an opportunity.

For a person with excuses,
every moment is a hassle.

Love is all about:

- Caring
- Compassion
- Forgiveness
- Giving
- Understanding
- Wisdom

People who face
challenges always
gain, gain, gain.

If we get away with
very little, we end
up with nothing.

If we are always in a giving mode, we are content and happy. If we are always in an expecting mode, we are dissatisfied and unhappy.

Create harmony and goodwill, in spite of obstacles.

Our only goal is to be an instrument of love, peace, and goodness.

Our good nature is a song of the heart.

We should make inner peace our constant companion.

Self-discipline is a long-term investment that pays great dividends.

The greatest sacrifice is to give up our ego feelings and ego images.

Humility and gratitude lead us to inner peace and goodwill.

Start each day with
positivity. End each day
with gratitude.

Simple living and high
thinking lead us to a
heavenly state.

Every good effort is a
solid brick we add to the
foundation of our life.